MARKS &
SPENCER

christmas

simple and delicious easy-to-make recipes

Mavis Young

Marks and Spencer p.l.c.
Baker Street, London, W1U 8EP

www.marksandspencer.com

Copyright © Exclusive Editions 2002

Titles in this series are subject to availability.

ISBN: 1–84273–844–5

Printed in China

Produced by the Bridgewater Book Company Ltd.

Photographer Calvey Taylor-Haw

Home Economist Ruth Pollock

The crockery featured on the following pages can be
purchased at Marks and Spencer's stores:

page 14 – silver-rimmed plate,
        02148/5302/119

page 24 – light green with yellow rim bowl & plate,
        02148/4923/108 & 02148/4925/108

NOTES FOR THE READER

- This book uses both metric and imperial measurements. Follow the same units of measurement throughout; do not mix metric and imperial.

- All spoon measurements are level: teaspoons are assumed to be 5 ml, and tablespoons are assumed to be 15 ml.

- Unless otherwise stated, milk is assumed to be full fat, eggs and individual vegetables such as potatoes are medium, and pepper is freshly ground black pepper.

- Recipes using raw or very lightly cooked eggs should be avoided by infants, the elderly, pregnant women, convalescents, and anyone suffering from an illness.

- The times given are an approximate guide only. Preparation times differ according to the techniques used by different people and the cooking times may also vary from those given. Optional ingredients, variations or serving suggestions have not been included in the calculations.

contents

introduction

Enjoying delicious food is an intrinsic part of Christmas. Where would we be without the seasonal delights of succulent turkey and cranberries, sweet mince pies, rich Christmas pudding and lashings of brandy butter? And who could imagine festivities without the party cheer of Christmas punch and the sweet spices of mulled wine?

This book features a dazzling array of festive recipes that will conjure up the cheer of the season wherever you happen to be. You'll find many traditional favourites here, such as roast turkey, Christmas pudding, mince pies and a sherry trifle. There are also contemporary and international dishes, such as Roast Turkey Oriental-Style and Mozzarella Crostini with Pesto & Caviar. Vegetarians will enjoy the Feta Cheese & Cranberry Tarts and the Mixed Nut Roast with Cranberry & Red Wine Sauce.

Christmas is a time for truly mouthwatering fare, whether you are entertaining a large group of people or curling up with home-made treats in front of a crackling fire. So, wherever you will be this Christmas, and whatever you are planning to do, there will be something here to suit the occasion.

guide to recipe key		
	very easy	Recipes are graded as follows: 1 pea = easy; 2 peas = very easy; 3 peas = extremely easy.
	serves 4	Recipes generally serve four people. Simply halve the ingredients to serve two, taking care not to mix metric and imperial measurements.
	10 minutes	Preparation time. Where marinating, chilling or cooling are involved, these times have been added on separately: e.g., 15 minutes + 30 minutes to marinate.
	10 minutes	Cooking time. Cooking times don't include the cooking of side dishes or accompaniments served with the main dishes.

salmon tartare
page 18

roast garlic potatoes
page 34

yuletide goose with honey & pears
page 54

white chocolate truffles
page 88

soups
& starters

Start your Christmas meal off with a swing
with this magnificent array of soups and
starters. In this chapter, tantalising
combinations of flavours, such as wild
mushrooms with sherry, and turkey and leek
with tarragon, make irresistible soups you
will want to savour again and again. If you
are entertaining a group of people, why
not impress them with a truly elegant
starter, such as the Salmon Tartare or the
Chèvre & Oyster Tartlets? Whatever you
choose, these dishes will delight everyone
and leave them longing for more.

wild mushroom & sherry soup

		ingredients	
very easy			
	2 tbsp olive oil	150 g/5$\frac{1}{2}$ oz mixed wild mushrooms	
	1 onion, chopped	600 ml/1 pint vegetable stock	
serves 4	1 garlic clove, chopped	350 ml/12 fl oz single cream	
	125 g/4$\frac{1}{2}$ oz sweet potato, peeled	4 tbsp sherry	
	and chopped	salt and pepper	
	1 leek, trimmed and sliced		
15 minutes	200 g/7 oz white and chestnut	TO GARNISH	
	mushrooms	Parmesan shavings	
		sautéed wild mushrooms, sliced	
35 minutes		fresh crusty rolls, to serve	

Heat the oil in a saucepan over a medium heat. Add the onion and garlic and cook, stirring, for 3 minutes until softened slightly. Add the sweet potato and cook for another 3 minutes. Stir in the leek and cook for another 2 minutes.

Stir in the mushrooms, stock and cream. Bring to the boil, then reduce the heat and simmer gently, stirring occasionally, for about 25 minutes. Remove from the heat, stir in the sherry, and leave to cool a little.

Transfer half of the soup into a food processor and blend until smooth. Return the mixture to the pan with the rest of the soup, season with salt and pepper and reheat gently, stirring. Pour into 4 warm soup bowls, garnish with Parmesan shavings and sliced wild mushrooms, and serve with fresh crusty rolls.

turkey, leek & stilton soup

		ingredients	
very easy	4 tbsp butter	150 ml/5 fl oz double cream	
	1 large onion, chopped	1 tbsp chopped fresh tarragon	
serves 4	1 leek, trimmed and sliced	pepper	
	325 g/11½ oz cooked turkey meat, sliced	GARNISH	
15 minutes	600 ml/1 pint chicken stock	fresh tarragon leaves	
	150 g/5½ oz Stilton cheese	croûtons	
25 minutes			

Melt the butter in a saucepan over a medium heat. Add the onion and cook, stirring, for 4 minutes, until slightly softened. Add the leek and cook for another 3 minutes.

Add the turkey to the pan and pour in the stock. Bring to the boil, then reduce the heat and simmer gently, stirring occasionally, for about 15 minutes. Remove from the heat and leave to cool a little.

Transfer half of the soup into a food processor and blend until smooth. Return the mixture to the pan with the rest of the soup, stir in the Stilton, cream and tarragon and season with pepper. Reheat gently, stirring. Remove from the heat, pour into 4 warm soup bowls, garnish with tarragon and croûtons and serve.

spiced pumpkin soup

	very easy	

ingredients

2 tbsp olive oil	1 bay leaf
1 onion, chopped	1 kg/2 lb 4 oz pumpkin, peeled,
1 garlic clove, chopped	deseeded and diced
1 tbsp chopped fresh root ginger	600 ml/1 pint vegetable stock
1 small red chilli, deseeded and	salt and pepper
finely chopped	
2 tbsp chopped fresh coriander	single cream, to garnish

very easy

serves 4

15 minutes

35 minutes

Heat the oil in a saucepan over a medium heat. Add the onion and garlic and cook, stirring, for about 4 minutes, until slightly softened. Add the ginger, chilli, coriander, bay leaf and pumpkin and cook for another 3 minutes.

Pour in the stock and bring to the boil. Using a slotted spoon, skim any scum from the surface. Reduce the heat and simmer gently, stirring occasionally, for about 25 minutes, or until the pumpkin is tender. Remove from the heat, take out the bay leaf and leave to cool a little.

Transfer the soup into a food processor and blend until smooth (you may have to do this in batches). Return the mixture to the pan and season with salt and pepper. Reheat gently, stirring. Remove from the heat, pour into 4 warm soup bowls, garnish each one with a swirl of cream and serve.

mozzarella crostini
with pesto & caviar

		ingredients	
very easy	8 slices white bread, crusts removed	PESTO	
	3 tbsp olive oil	75 g/2¾ oz fresh basil, finely chopped	
serves 4	200 g/7 oz mozzarella, cut into thin pieces	35 g/1¼ oz pine kernels, finely chopped	
	6 tbsp lumpfish caviar	2 garlic cloves, finely chopped	
20 minutes		3 tbsp olive oil	
15 minutes			

Preheat the oven to 180°C/350°F/Gas Mark 4. Using a sharp knife, cut the bread into fancy shapes, such as half-moons, stars and Christmas trees. Drizzle with oil, transfer to an ovenproof dish and cook in the preheated oven for 15 minutes.

While the bread is cooking, make the pesto. Put the basil, pine kernels and garlic into a small bowl. Pour in the olive oil and stir together well.

Remove the bread shapes from the oven and leave to cool. Spread a layer of pesto on the shapes, top each one with a piece of mozzarella and some caviar and serve.

olive tapenade toasts

		ingredients	
	very easy	1 large baguette (preferably 1 day old), cut into diagonal slices 2 tbsp olive oil	TAPENADE 150 g/5½ oz black olives, stoned 3 canned anchovy fillets, drained 1 garlic clove, chopped 2 tbsp blanched almonds, chopped 4 tbsp olive oil 1 tsp lemon juice salt and pepper
	serves 4		
	15 minutes		
	15 minutes		

Preheat the oven to 180°C/350°F/Gas Mark 4. Spread the baguette slices with oil, put them into an ovenproof dish and cook in the preheated oven for 15 minutes.

While the bread is cooking, make the tapenade. Put the olives, anchovies, garlic and almonds into a food processor and blend until combined. With the motor running, slowly pour in the olive oil through the feed tube, then add the lemon juice. Season with salt and pepper and transfer to a bowl. Cover with clingfilm and refrigerate until needed.

Remove the bread shapes from the oven and allow to cool. Spread each piece with tapenade and serve.

salmon tartare

	ingredients	
very easy	500 g/1lb 2 oz salmon fillet, skin removed	TOPPING
	2 tbsp sea salt	400 g/14 oz cream cheese
serves 4	1 tbsp caster sugar	1 tbsp chopped fresh chives
	2 tbsp chopped fresh dill	pinch of paprika
20 minutes + 48 hours to marinate	pepper	sprigs of fresh dill, to garnish
	1 tbsp chopped fresh tarragon	
	1 tsp Dijon mustard	
—	juice of 1 lemon	

Put the salmon into a shallow glass dish. Combine the sea salt, sugar and dill, then rub the mixture into the fish until well coated. Season with plenty of pepper. Cover with clingfilm and refrigerate for at least 48 hours, turning the salmon once.

When ready to serve, put the chopped tarragon into a mixing bowl with the mustard and lemon juice. Season well. Remove the salmon from the refrigerator, chop into small pieces then add to the bowl. Stir until the salmon is well coated.

To make the topping, put the cream cheese, chives and paprika into a separate bowl and mix well. Place a 10-cm/4-inch steel cooking ring or round biscuit cutter on each of 4 small serving plates. Divide the salmon between the four steel rings so that each ring is half-full. Level the surface of each one, then top with the cream cheese mixture. Smooth the surfaces, then carefully remove the steel rings. Garnish with sprigs of fresh dill and serve.

chèvre & oyster tartlets

	ingredients	
very easy	125 g/4½ oz plain flour, plus extra for dusting	1 onion, chopped
		12 oysters, cleaned
makes 12	pinch of salt	2 tbsp chopped fresh parsley
	100 g/3½ oz butter, chopped, plus extra for greasing	salt and pepper
		200 g/7 oz goat's cheese, crumbled
20 minutes + 45 minutes to chill	1 egg yolk	sprigs of fresh flat-leaved parsley, to garnish
20 minutes		

Sift the flour and salt together in a bowl. Rub in 90 g/3¼ oz of the butter, then mix in the egg yolk to make a dough. Add a little cold water if needed. Shape into a ball and turn out onto a lightly floured work surface. Roll out to a thickness of 5 mm/¼ inch. Grease 12 small tartlet tins, about 7 cm/2¾ inches in diameter, with butter. Line the tins with dough and trim the edges. Chill in the refrigerator for 45 minutes to prevent the pastry shrinking.

Preheat the oven to 200°C/400°F/Gas Mark 6. Bake the tartlet shells for 10 minutes until golden. Meanwhile, heat the remaining butter over a medium heat, add the onion and cook for 4 minutes, stirring. Take the oysters out of their shells, add to the pan with the parsley, season, and cook for 1 minute. Remove the tartlets from the oven. Divide 100 g/3½ oz of the goat's cheese between them. Top with the oyster mixture, crumble over the remaining cheese, then bake for 10 minutes. Garnish with fresh parsley and serve hot.

light meals, snacks & side dishes

Christmas is not always just one big feast, but rather a series of special meals over several days. When lighter meals are required, what better way to keep the spirit of Christmas going than with a selection of festive snacks? This chapter contains some delicious mini-feasts, such as Turkey Tortillas with Soured Cream, which provide a practical way of using any left-over turkey. The chapter finishes with a tempting selection of vegetable accompaniments that will prove a tasty addition to the Christmas meal or to any light supper.

spiced apple, brie & rocket salad

very easy	
serves 4	
15 minutes	
20 minutes	

ingredients

500 ml/18 fl oz red wine
100 g/3½ oz sugar
1 cinnamon stick
1 tbsp grated fresh root ginger
4 large apples
2 tbsp lemon juice
150 g/5½ oz rocket leaves
150 g/5½ oz Brie, cubed
salt and pepper

DRESSING
3 tbsp red wine vinegar
125 ml/4 fl oz extra-virgin olive oil
1 tbsp honey

Put the wine, sugar, cinnamon and ginger into a large saucepan and bring to the boil. Reduce the heat and simmer gently for 10 minutes. Core and slice the apples, and brush with lemon juice. Add the apple slices to the pan and cook for another 10 minutes. Remove from the heat and leave to cool completely.

To make the dressing, put the vinegar, olive oil and honey into a glass jar, screw on the lid and shake well. Alternatively, put the ingredients into a small bowl and whisk together.

To assemble the salad, put the rocket leaves in the bottom of a salad bowl. Drain the apples well and scatter them over the rocket, then top with Brie and season with salt and pepper. Drizzle over the dressing, toss the salad until well coated and serve.

monkfish parcels

	ingredients	

very easy	4 tsp olive oil
	2 courgettes, trimmed and sliced
	1 large red pepper, skinned, deseeded
	  and cut into strips
	2 monkfish fillets, about 125 g/4½ oz
	  each, skin and membrane removed
		6 rashers smoked streaky bacon
		salt and pepper
		
		TO SERVE
		freshly cooked pasta
		slices of fresh olive bread

serves 4		
15 minutes		
25 minutes		

Preheat the oven to 190°C/375°F/Gas Mark 5. Cut out 4 large pieces of foil, about 23 cm/9 inches square. Brush them lightly with oil, then divide the courgettes and red pepper between them.

Rinse the fish fillets under cold running water and pat dry with kitchen paper. Cut them in half, then place one piece on top of each pile of courgettes and red pepper. Cut the bacon rashers in half, and lay 3 pieces across each piece of fish. Season with salt and pepper, drizzle over the remaining oil and close up the parcels. Seal tightly, transfer to an ovenproof dish, and bake in the preheated oven for 25 minutes.

Remove from the oven, open each foil parcel slightly, and serve with freshly cooked pasta and slices of fresh olive bread.

turkey tortillas
with soured cream

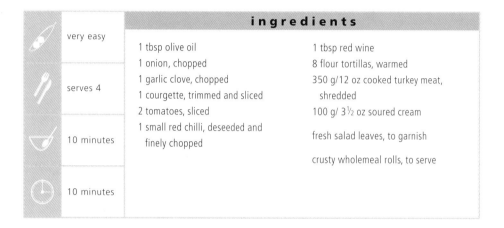

		ingredients	
very easy	1 tbsp olive oil	1 tbsp red wine
	1 onion, chopped	8 flour tortillas, warmed
serves 4	1 garlic clove, chopped	350 g/12 oz cooked turkey meat,
	1 courgette, trimmed and sliced	shredded
	2 tomatoes, sliced	100 g/ 3½ oz soured cream
10 minutes	1 small red chilli, deseeded and	fresh salad leaves, to garnish
	finely chopped	
		crusty wholemeal rolls, to serve
10 minutes		

Heat the oil in a frying pan over a medium heat. Add the onion,
garlic and courgette and cook, stirring, for 4 minutes. Add the
tomatoes, chilli and red wine, cook for another 5 minutes, then
remove from the heat.

Arrange the warmed tortillas on a clean work surface and spoon
some tomato mixture onto each one. Add some shredded turkey
and a spoonful of soured cream, then roll up the tortillas and
arrange them on serving plates. Garnish with salad leaves and
serve with crusty wholemeal rolls.

honeyed parsnips

		ingredients
	very easy	8 parsnips, peeled and quartered
	serves 4	4 tbsp vegetable oil
		1 tbsp honey
	5 minutes	
	50 minutes	

Preheat the oven to 180°C/350°F/Gas Mark 4.

Bring a large saucepan of water to the boil. Reduce the heat, add the parsnips and cook for 5 minutes. Drain thoroughly.

Pour 2 tablespoons of the oil into a shallow, ovenproof dish and add the parsnips. Mix the remaining oil with the honey and drizzle over the parsnips. Roast in the preheated oven for 45 minutes until golden brown and tender. Remove from the oven and serve.

spiced winter vegetables

very easy	
serves 4	
15 minutes	
1 hour 10 minutes	

ingredients

2 large baking potatoes, scrubbed but
  left unpeeled
2 parsnips, scrubbed and trimmed but
  left unpeeled
4 large carrots

1 garlic clove, finely chopped
6 tbsp chilli oil or extra-virgin olive oil
$\frac{1}{2}$ tsp mild chilli powder
pinch of paprika
salt and pepper

Preheat the oven to 220°C/425°F/Gas Mark 7. Bring a large saucepan of water to the boil.

Cut the potatoes and parsnips into wedges. Cut the carrots lengthways and then diagonally into large pieces of a similar size to the potato and parsnip wedges. Add the vegetables to the pan and cook for 10 minutes. Drain thoroughly and leave to cool.

Put the garlic, oil, chilli powder and paprika into a jug or small bowl and mix together well. Transfer the vegetables to an ovenproof dish and pour over the oil mixture. Season with salt and pepper. Turn the vegetables in the oil until thoroughly coated. Roast in the preheated oven for at least 1 hour, or until golden brown and tender. Remove from the oven and serve.

roast garlic potatoes

very easy	
serves 4	
10 minutes	
50 minutes	

ingredients

600 g/1 lb 5 oz small new potatoes, scrubbed
2 garlic cloves, chopped
3 tbsp olive oil

½ tsp salt
pinch of paprika
pepper

Preheat the oven to 200°C/400°F/Gas Mark 6. Arrange the potatoes in a roasting tin.

Put the garlic into a small jug or bowl. Add the oil, salt, paprika and pepper and mix together well. Pour the oil mixture over the potatoes, then turn the potatoes in the mixture until thoroughly coated. Roast in the preheated oven for 50 minutes, basting occasionally, until golden brown and tender. Remove from the oven and serve.

honey-glazed red cabbage
with sultanas

	ingredients	
very easy	2 tbsp butter	1 tbsp honey
	1 garlic clove, chopped	100 ml/3½ fl oz red wine
serves 4	650 g/1 lb 7 oz red cabbage, shredded	100 ml/3½ fl oz water
	150 g/5½ oz sultanas	
10 minutes		
50 minutes		

Melt the butter in a large saucepan over a medium heat. Add the garlic and cook, stirring, for 1 minute, until slightly softened.

Add the cabbage and sultanas, then stir in the honey. Cook for another minute. Pour in the wine and water and bring to the boil. Reduce the heat, cover and simmer, stirring occasionally, for about 45 minutes or until the cabbage is cooked. Serve hot.

brussels sprouts
with buttered chestnuts

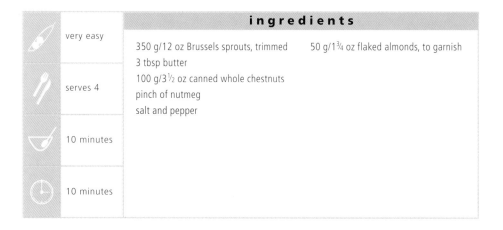

	ingredients
very easy	350 g/12 oz Brussels sprouts, trimmed 50 g/1¾ oz flaked almonds, to garnish
	3 tbsp butter
serves 4	100 g/3½ oz canned whole chestnuts
	pinch of nutmeg
	salt and pepper
10 minutes	
10 minutes	

Bring a large saucepan of salted water to the boil. Add the Brussels sprouts and cook for 5 minutes. Drain thoroughly.

Melt the butter in a large saucepan over a medium heat. Add the Brussels sprouts and cook, stirring, for 3 minutes, then add the chestnuts and nutmeg. Season with salt and pepper and stir well. Cook for another 2 minutes, stirring, then remove from the heat. Transfer to a serving dish, scatter over the almonds and serve.

garlic mushrooms with
white wine & chestnuts

		ingredients	
very easy	4 tbsp butter	salt and pepper
	4 garlic cloves, chopped	300 g/10½ oz canned whole chestnuts
serves 4	200 g/7 oz button mushrooms, sliced	100 g/3½ oz chanterelle mushrooms,
	200 g/7 oz chestnut mushrooms, sliced	sliced
	4 tbsp dry white wine	
15 minutes	100 ml/3½ fl oz double cream	chopped fresh parsley, to garnish
10 minutes		

Melt the butter in a large saucepan over a medium heat. Add the garlic and cook, stirring, for 3 minutes, until softened. Add the button and chestnut mushrooms and cook for another 3 minutes.

Stir in the wine and cream and season with salt and pepper. Cook for 2 minutes, stirring, then add the chestnuts and the chanterelle mushrooms. Cook for another 2 minutes, stirring, then remove from the heat and transfer to a serving dish. Garnish with chopped fresh parsley and serve.

main courses

Transform your Christmas meal into a veritable banquet with the stunning display of dishes in this chapter. From Roast Turkey, Yuletide Goose and succulent Duck with Blueberries to Redcurrant-glazed Ham and a mouthwatering selection of sauces, there is something to tempt everyone. The Herbed Salmon with Hollandaise Sauce will delight fish-lovers, and delicious, meat-free recipes such as a festive Nut Roast and Feta Cheese & Cranberry Tarts will have the vegetarians among you coming back for more.

mixed nut roast with cranberry & red wine sauce

easy	
serves 4	
30 minutes	
35 minutes	

ingredients

2 tbsp butter, plus extra for greasing
2 garlic cloves, chopped
1 large onion, chopped
50 g/1¾ oz pine kernels, toasted
75 g/2¾ oz hazelnuts, toasted
50 g/1¾ oz walnuts, ground
50 g/1¾ oz cashew nuts, ground
100 g/3½ oz wholemeal breadcrumbs
1 egg, lightly beaten
2 tbsp chopped fresh thyme
250 ml/9 fl oz vegetable stock

salt and pepper

CRANBERRY & RED WINE SAUCE
175 g/6 oz fresh cranberries
100 g/3½ oz caster sugar
300 ml/10 fl oz red wine
1 cinnamon stick

sprigs of fresh thyme, to garnish

Brussels Sprouts with Buttered
    Chestnuts (see page 38), to serve

Preheat the oven to 180°C/350°F/Gas Mark 4. Grease a loaf tin and line it with greaseproof paper. Melt the butter in a saucepan over a medium heat. Add the garlic and onion and cook, stirring, for about 3 minutes. Remove the pan from the heat. Grind the pine kernels and hazelnuts. Stir all the nuts into the pan and add the breadcrumbs, egg, thyme, stock and seasoning.

Spoon the mixture into the loaf tin and level the surface. Cook in the centre of the preheated oven for 30 minutes or until cooked through and golden. The loaf is cooked when a skewer inserted into the centre comes out clean. Halfway through the cooking time, make the sauce. Put all the ingredients in a saucepan and bring to the boil. Reduce the heat and simmer, stirring occasionally, for 15 minutes.

To serve, remove the sauce from the heat and discard the cinnamon stick. Remove the nut roast from the oven and turn out. Garnish with thyme; serve with the sauce and Brussels sprouts.

feta cheese & cranberry tarts

		ingredients	
easy		4 tbsp olive oil	8 sheets of filo pastry, cut into
		1 onion, chopped	16 squares measuring 13 cm/
serves 4		8 black olives, stoned and chopped	5 inches across
		85 g/3 oz cranberries	125 g/4½ oz feta cheese (drained
		1 eating apple	weight), cut into small cubes
20 minutes		1 tbsp lemon juice	
15 minutes			

Preheat the oven to 180°C/350°F/Gas Mark 4. Heat 2 tablespoons of oil in a frying pan over a medium heat. Add the onion and cook, stirring, for 3 minutes, until slightly softened. Remove from the heat and stir in the olives and cranberries. Core and chop the apple and add it to the pan with the lemon juice. Stir well and set aside.

Brush the filo squares with the remaining oil and use them to line 4 small flan tins. Place 4 sheets in each tin, staggering them so that the overhanging corners make a decorative star shape.

Divide the cranberry filling between the four pastry cases. Scatter over the feta cheese and bake in the centre of the preheated oven for about 10 minutes until golden. Serve hot.

herbed salmon
with hollandaise sauce

	ingredients	
easy	4 salmon fillets, about 175 g/6 oz each, skin removed	salt and pepper
		225 g/8 oz butter, cut into small cubes
serves 4	salt and pepper	juice of 1 lemon
	2 tbsp olive oil	
	1 tbsp chopped fresh dill	chopped fresh chives, to garnish
	1 tbsp chopped fresh chives	
15 minutes		TO SERVE
	HOLLANDAISE SAUCE	freshly boiled new potatoes
	3 egg yolks	freshly cooked mangetouts
8–10 minutes	1 tbsp water	

Preheat the grill to medium. Rinse the fish fillets under cold running water and pat dry with kitchen paper. Season with salt and pepper. Combine the olive oil with the dill and chives, then brush the mixture over the fish. Transfer to the grill and cook for about 6–8 minutes, turning once and brushing with more oil and herb mixture, until cooked to your taste.

Meanwhile, to make the sauce, put the egg yolks in a heatproof bowl over a pan of boiling water (or use a double boiler). Add the water and season with salt and pepper. Lower the heat and simmer, whisking constantly, until the mixture begins to thicken. Whisk in the butter, cube by cube, until the mixture is thick and shiny. Whisk in the lemon juice, then remove from the heat.

Remove the fish from the grill and transfer to individual serving plates. Pour over the sauce and garnish with chopped fresh chives. Serve with freshly boiled new potatoes and mangetouts.

traditional roast turkey with wine & mushrooms

		ingredients
easy	3–3.5 kg/6½–7¾ lb oven-ready turkey 6 tbsp olive oil 1 garlic clove, finely chopped 100 ml/3½ fl oz red wine	2 tbsp finely chopped fresh sage 1 tbsp lemon juice salt and pepper
serves 4	STUFFING 100 g/3½ oz white mushrooms 1 onion, chopped 6 tbsp butter	PORT & CRANBERRY SAUCE 100 g/3½ oz sugar 250 ml/9 fl oz port 175 g/6 oz fresh cranberries
25 minutes	1 garlic clove, chopped 100 g/3½ oz fresh breadcrumbs	TO SERVE Roast Garlic Potatoes (see page 34) Spiced Winter Vegetables (see page 32)
3 hours + 25 minutes		

Preheat the oven to 200°C/400°F/Gas Mark 6. To make the stuffing, clean and chop the mushrooms, put them in a pan with the onion and butter and cook for 3 minutes. Remove from the heat and stir in the other ingredients. Rinse the turkey, pat dry with kitchen paper, fill the neck end with stuffing and truss with string.

Pour the oil into a roasting dish and put the turkey in it. Rub the garlic over the bird and pour the wine over. Roast for 20 minutes. Baste, reduce the heat to 190°C/375°F/Gas Mark 5 and roast for 40 minutes. Baste again; cover with foil. Roast for 2 hours, basting regularly. Check that the bird is cooked by inserting a knife between the legs and body. If the juices run clear, it is cooked. Remove from the oven; leave to stand for 25 minutes. Meanwhile, put the sugar, port and cranberries into a pan. Warm over a medium heat until almost boiling. Reduce the heat, simmer for 15 minutes, stirring, then remove from the heat. Serve with the turkey and vegetables.

roast turkey oriental-style

easy	
serves 4	
20 minutes	
3 hours + 25 minutes	

ingredients

3–3.5 kg/6½–7¾ lb oven-ready turkey
6 tbsp olive oil
1 tbsp lime juice

STUFFING
2 spring onions, trimmed and chopped
1 large garlic clove, chopped
2 tbsp sesame oil
1 lemon grass stalk, about 7 cm/
    2¾ inches long
1 tbsp grated fresh root ginger
1 small red chilli, deseeded, chopped

2 tbsp chopped fresh kaffir lime leaves
juice of 1 lime
1 tbsp rice wine
salt and pepper

TO GARNISH
wedges of fresh lime
fresh coriander, chopped

TO SERVE
freshly boiled jasmine rice
freshly cooked seasonal vegetables

Preheat the oven to 200°C/400°F/Gas Mark 6. To make the stuffing, cook the onions and garlic in the sesame oil over a low heat for 2 minutes. Remove from the heat and stir in the other ingredients, seasoned to taste. Rinse the turkey and pat dry with kitchen paper. Fill the neck end of the turkey with stuffing and truss with string.

Pour 4 tablespoons of olive oil into a large roasting dish and place the turkey in it. Mix the lime juice with the remaining oil and brush all over the turkey. Roast for 20 minutes. Baste the turkey, reduce the heat to 190°C/375°F/Gas Mark 5 and roast for 40 minutes. Baste again and cover with foil. Roast for 2 hours, basting regularly. Check that the bird is cooked by inserting a knife between the legs and body. If the juices run clear, it is cooked. Remove from the oven and leave to stand for 25 minutes. Serve the turkey with jasmine rice and vegetables, garnished with lime wedges and coriander.

yuletide goose
with honey & pears

		ingredients	
easy		3.5–4.5 kg/7¾–10 lb oven-ready goose	TO SERVE Roast Garlic Potatoes (see page 34)
serves 4		1 tsp salt 4 pears 1 tbsp lemon juice 4 tbsp butter 2 tbsp honey	Spiced Winter Vegetables (see page 32) Brussels Sprouts with Buttered Chestnuts (see page 38) Honey-Glazed Red Cabbage with Sultanas (see page 36)
20 minutes		lemon slices, to garnish	
3–3½ hours			

Preheat the oven to 220°C/425°F/Gas Mark 7. Rinse the goose and pat dry. Use a fork to prick the skin all over, then rub with salt. Place the bird upside down on a rack in a roasting tin. Roast for 30 minutes. Drain off the fat. Turn the bird over and roast for 15 minutes. Drain off the fat. Reduce the heat to 180°C/350°F/ Gas Mark 4 and roast for 15 minutes per 450 g/1 lb. Cover with foil 15 minutes before the end of the cooking time. Check that the bird is cooked by inserting a knife between the legs and body. If the juices run clear, it is cooked. Remove from the oven.

Peel and halve the pears and brush with lemon juice. Melt the butter and honey in a pan over a low heat, then add the pears. Cook, stirring, for 5–10 minutes, until tender. Remove from the heat, arrange the pears around the goose and pour the sweet juices over the bird. Garnish with lemon slices and serve with garlic potatoes, winter vegetables, Brussels sprouts and red cabbage.

sliced duck breast
with madeira & blueberries

		ingredients	
easy			
serves 4	6 duck breasts (skin left on) 1 garlic clove, chopped grated rind and juice of 1 orange 1 tbsp chopped fresh parsley salt and pepper	TO GARNISH blueberries orange slices TO SERVE	
15 minutes + 1 hour to marinate	MADEIRA & BLUEBERRY SAUCE 150 g/5$\frac{1}{2}$ oz blueberries 250 ml/9 fl oz Madeira 1 tbsp redcurrant jelly	roast potatoes selection of freshly cooked vegetables	
15 minutes			

Use a sharp knife to make several shallow diagonal cuts in each duck breast. Put the duck in a glass bowl with the garlic, orange and parsley. Season, and stir well. Turn the duck in the mixture until thoroughly coated. Cover with clingfilm and leave in the refrigerator to marinate for at least 1 hour.

Heat a dry, non-stick frying pan over a medium heat. Add the duck breasts and cook for 4 minutes, then turn them over and cook for a further 4 minutes or according to taste. Remove from the heat, cover the pan, and leave to stand for 5 minutes.

Halfway through the cooking time, put the blueberries, Madeira and redcurrant jelly into a separate pan. Bring to the boil. Reduce the heat and simmer for 10 minutes, then remove from the heat.

Transfer the duck to serving plates and garnish with blueberries and orange slices. Serve with roast potatoes, a selection of freshly cooked vegetables and the Madeira and blueberry sauce.

redcurrant-glazed ham
with madeira sauce

		ingredients	
easy			
serves 4	2 kg/4 lb 8 oz lean gammon 4 cloves 6 tbsp redcurrant jelly 1 tbsp wholegrain mustard 3 tbsp Madeira grated rind and juice of 1 orange grated rind and juice of 1 lemon	TO GARNISH orange slices lemon slices TO SERVE Honey-Glazed Red Cabbage with Sultanas (see page 36) freshly cooked French beans freshly boiled new potatoes
15 minutes			
2 ½ hours			

Bring a large saucepan of water to the boil. Reduce the heat and add the gammon and the cloves. Cover and simmer for 1 hour, topping up the water level when necessary.

Preheat the oven to 180°C/350°F/Gas Mark 4. Remove the gammon from the heat, drain and remove the skin. Place the meat, fat side up, on a rack in a roasting dish. Using a sharp knife, score the fat on the ham. Mix 2 tablespoons of redcurrant jelly with the mustard, then rub it into the scored skin. Cook in the preheated oven for 1 ½ hours, or until cooked through. About 5 minutes before the end of the cooking time, put the remaining redcurrant jelly in a small pan with the Madeira and the citrus rind and juice. Warm gently over a low heat and simmer, stirring, for 5 minutes.

Remove the gammon from the oven, transfer to serving plates and garnish with citrus slices. Serve with the Madeira sauce, new potatoes, French beans and red cabbage.

sweet & sour glazed pork

		ingredients	
easy	1 kg/2 lb 4 oz pork loin, backbone removed and rind scored	100 g/3½ oz white mushrooms, chopped	
serves 4	salt and pepper 6 tbsp honey 1 tbsp wine vinegar 1 tsp soy sauce 1 tsp Dijon mustard	100 g/3½ oz fresh breadcrumbs 2 tbsp finely chopped fresh sage 1 tbsp lemon juice salt and pepper	
20 minutes		fresh sage leaves, to garnish	
1 hour 40 minutes	STUFFING 6 tbsp butter 1 onion, chopped	TO SERVE Roast Garlic Potatoes (see page 34) Spiced Winter Vegetables (see page 32)	

Preheat the oven to 230°C/450°F/Gas Mark 8. To make the stuffing, melt the butter in a pan over a medium heat. Add the onion and cook, stirring, for about 3 minutes, until softened. Add the mushrooms and cook for another 2 minutes. Remove from the heat and stir in the breadcrumbs, sage, lemon juice and seasoning.

Put the stuffing in the middle of the pork loin, then roll up and tie the loin with several pieces of string. Place the joint in a roasting tin, rub the skin with plenty of salt and season with pepper. In a small bowl, mix together the honey, vinegar, soy sauce and mustard. Pour the mixture over the pork.

Cook in the preheated oven for 20 minutes, then reduce the heat to 180°C/350°F/Gas Mark 4 and cook, basting from time to time, for about 1¼ hours, or until cooked through. Remove from the oven and leave to stand for 15 minutes. Garnish with fresh sage leaves and serve with garlic potatoes and winter vegetables.

hazelnut crusted lamb

		ingredients	
easy		8 best end of neck lamb cutlets, excess fat removed	2 tbsp chopped fresh thyme
			6 tbsp basil oil
serves 4		salt and pepper	
		6 tbsp flour	sprigs of fresh thyme, to garnish
		2 eggs, beaten	
		175 g/6 oz fresh white or wholemeal breadcrumbs	TO SERVE
20 minutes			Roast Garlic Potatoes (see page 34)
		75 g/2¾ oz hazelnuts, lightly toasted and chopped	fresh salad leaves
10 minutes		2 tbsp chopped fresh parsley	

Season the lamb cutlets on both sides with salt and pepper. Put the flour on a large plate, and place the beaten eggs in a large bowl. Take another large bowl and mix together the breadcrumbs, hazelnuts and herbs. Season well.

Turn the lamb cutlets in the flour, dip them in the eggs, then coat well in the hazelnut mixture. Heat the oil in a frying pan over a medium heat. Add the cutlets to the pan and cook for 5 minutes, then turn them over and cook on the other side for another 5 minutes (you may need to do this in batches). Lift out of the pan and transfer to serving plates. Garnish with sprigs of thyme and serve with garlic potatoes and fresh salad leaves.

festive beef wellington

		ingredients	
easy		750 g/1 lb 10 oz thick beef fillet	1 egg, beaten
		2 tbsp butter	
		salt and pepper	chopped fresh sage, to garnish
serves 4		2 tbsp vegetable oil	
		1 garlic clove, chopped	TO SERVE
		1 onion, chopped	Roast Garlic Potatoes (see page 34)
20 minutes		175 g/6 oz chestnut mushrooms	Garlic Mushrooms with White Wine
		1 tbsp chopped fresh sage	and Chestnuts (see page 40)
		salt and pepper	freshly cooked Brussels sprouts
1 hour 10 minutes		350 g/12 oz frozen puff pastry, defrosted	

Preheat the oven to 220°C/425°F/Gas Mark 7. Put the beef in a roasting tin, spread with butter and season. Roast for 30 minutes, then remove from the oven. Meanwhile, heat the oil in a pan over a medium heat. Add the garlic and onion and cook, stirring, for 3 minutes. Stir in the mushrooms, sage and seasoning and cook for 5 minutes. Remove from the heat.

Roll out the pastry into a rectangle large enough to enclose the beef, then place the beef in the middle and spread the mushroom mixture over it. Bring the long sides of the pastry together over the beef and seal with beaten egg. Tuck the short ends over (trim away excess pastry) and seal. Place on a baking sheet, seam-side down. Make 2 slits in the top. Decorate with dough shapes and brush with beaten egg. Bake for 40 minutes. If the pastry browns too quickly, cover with foil. Remove from the oven, garnish with sage, and serve with garlic potatoes, garlic mushrooms and sprouts.

roast pheasant with
red wine & herbs

		ingredients
easy	100 g/3½ oz butter, slightly softened	TO SERVE
	1 tbsp chopped fresh thyme	Honeyed Parsnips (see page 30)
	1 tbsp chopped fresh parsley	sautéed potatoes
serves 4	2 oven-ready young pheasants	freshly cooked Brussels sprouts
	salt and pepper	
	4 tbsp vegetable oil	
20 minutes	125 ml/4 fl oz red wine	
1 hour		

Preheat the oven to 190°C/375°F/Gas Mark 5. Put the butter into a small bowl and mix in the chopped herbs. Lift the skins off the pheasants, taking care not to tear them, and push the herb butter under the skins. Season with salt and pepper. Pour the oil into a roasting tin, add the pheasants and cook in the preheated oven for 45 minutes, basting occasionally. Remove from the oven, pour over the red wine, then return to the oven and cook for another 15 minutes, or until cooked through. Check that each bird is cooked by inserting a knife between the legs and body. If the juices run clear, they are cooked.

Remove the pheasants from the oven, cover with foil and leave to stand for 15 minutes. Divide between individual serving plates, and serve with honeyed parsnips, sautéed potatoes and freshly cooked Brussels sprouts.

roast venison with brandy sauce

easy

serves 4

15 minutes

2 hours

ingredients

6 tbsp vegetable oil
salt and pepper
1 saddle of fresh venison

BRANDY SAUCE
4 tbsp vegetable stock
1 tbsp plain flour
175 ml/6 fl oz brandy
100 ml/3 ½ fl oz double cream

sprigs of fresh thyme, to garnish

TO SERVE
Roast Garlic Potatoes (see page 34)
Honeyed Parsnips (see page 30)
selection of freshly cooked vegetables

Preheat the oven to 180°C/350°F/Gas Mark 4. Heat 3 tablespoons of the oil in a frying pan over a high heat. Season the venison, then cook it in the pan over a high heat until lightly browned all over. Pour the remaining oil into a roasting pan. Add the venison, cover with foil and roast, basting occasionally, for about 1 ½ hours or until cooked through. Remove from the oven and transfer the venison to a serving platter. Cover with foil and set aside.

To make the sauce, pour the stock into the roasting pan and heat it on the hob, stirring to loosen browned bits of food from the bottom. Stir in the flour and cook for 1 minute. Gradually stir in the brandy, bring to the boil, then reduce the heat and simmer, stirring, for 10–15 minutes until the sauce has thickened a little. Remove from the heat and stir in the cream.

Garnish the venison with thyme and serve with garlic potatoes, honeyed parsnips, a selection of vegetables and the brandy sauce.

desserts, sweets & drinks

The truly spectacular desserts in this chapter are guaranteed to finish any meal with a flourish. Whether your passion is Fruit Compôte with Port & Whipped Cream, Fresh Figs & Brandy Butter, Christmas Pudding or a hearty slice of Christmas Cake, there will be something here to tempt you. For a lighter dessert, why not try the Brandy & Orange Ice Cream? And if you can find a little room for more, try rounding off your meal with White Chocolate Truffles, Mulled Wine or Spiced Hot Chocolate.

festive sherry trifle

	ingredients	
easy	FRUIT LAYER	CUSTARD LAYER
	100 g/3½ oz trifle sponges	6 egg yolks
serves 4	150 ml/5 fl oz raspberry jam	50 g/1¾ oz caster sugar
	250 ml/9 fl oz sherry	500 ml/18 fl oz milk
	150 g/5½ oz frozen raspberries,	1 tsp vanilla essence
15 minutes	defrosted	
+ 6 hours to	400 g/14 oz canned mixed fruit,	TOPPING
soak/chill	drained	300 ml/10 fl oz double cream
	1 large banana, sliced	1–2 tbsp caster sugar
2–3 minutes		toasted mixed nuts, chopped,
		to decorate

Spread the trifle sponges with jam, cut them into bite-sized cubes and arrange in the bottom of a large glass serving bowl. Pour over the sherry and leave for 30 minutes.

Combine the raspberries, canned fruit and banana and arrange over the sponges. Cover with clingfilm and chill for 30 minutes.

To make the custard, put the egg yolks and sugar into a bowl and whisk together. Pour the milk into a pan and warm gently over a low heat. Remove from the heat and gradually stir into the egg mixture, then return the mixture to the pan and stir constantly over a low heat until thickened. Do not boil. Remove from the heat, pour into a bowl and stir in the vanilla. Cool for 1 hour. Spread the custard over the trifle, cover with clingfilm and chill for 2 hours.

To make the topping, whip the cream in a bowl and stir in sugar to taste. Spread over the trifle, then scatter over the nuts. Cover with clingfilm and refrigerate for at least 2 hours before serving.

fruit compôte with
port & whipped cream

		ingredients	
very easy	1 tbsp butter	TOPPING
	200 g/7 oz blueberries	450 ml/16 fl oz double cream
serves 4	200 g/7 oz blackberries	3–4 tbsp caster sugar
	100 g/3½ oz strawberries, hulled	
	6 tbsp port	grated chocolate, to decorate
15 minutes + 30 minutes to cool	3 tbsp blueberry jam	
	1 tbsp cornflour	
	1 tsp mixed spice	
15 minutes		

Preheat the oven to 190°C/375°F/Gas Mark 5. Grease a baking dish with butter and add all the fruit.

In a bowl, mix together the port, jam, cornflour and mixed spice. Pour the mixture over the fruit and mix well. Bake in the preheated oven for 15 minutes, stirring from time to time. Remove from the oven and leave to cool to room temperature, then divide between 4 decorative serving glasses.

For the topping, whip the cream in a mixing bowl and stir in sugar to taste. Spoon the mixture over the fruit, top with grated chocolate and serve.

christmas pudding

		ingredients	
easy	200 g/7 oz currants	50 g/1¾ oz blanched almonds,
	200 g/7 oz raisins	chopped
	200 g/7 oz sultanas	juice of 1 orange
serves 4	150 ml/5 fl oz sweet sherry	grated rind of ½ orange
	175 g/6 oz butter, plus extra	grated rind of ½ lemon
2¼ hours +	for greasing	½ tsp ground mixed spice
2–8 weeks	175 g/6 oz brown sugar	
to chill	4 eggs, beaten	holly leaves, to decorate
	150 g/5½ oz self-raising flour	
8 hours	100 g/3½ oz fresh white or	
	wholemeal breadcrumbs	

Put the currants, raisins and sultanas into a glass bowl and pour over the sherry. Leave to soak for at least 2 hours.

Mix the butter and sugar in a bowl. Beat in the eggs, then fold in the flour. Stir in the soaked fruit and sherry with the breadcrumbs, almonds, orange juice and rind, lemon rind and mixed spice. Grease a pudding basin and press the mixture into it, leaving a gap of 2.5 cm/1 inch at the top. Cut a circle of greaseproof paper 3 cm/1¼ inches larger than the top of the basin, grease with butter and place over the pudding. Secure with string, then top with 2 layers of foil. Place the pudding in a pan filled with boiling water which reaches two-thirds of the way up the basin. Reduce the heat and simmer for 6 hours, topping up the water when necessary.

Remove from the heat and leave to cool. Renew the greaseproof paper and foil and refrigerate for 2–8 weeks. To reheat, steam for 2 hours as before. Decorate with holly and serve.

fresh figs & brandy butter

		ingredients	
	extremely easy	115 g/4 oz butter, slightly softened	fresh mint leaves, to decorate
	serves 4	50 g/1¾ oz icing sugar	
		1 tbsp brandy	
	10 minutes	12 fresh figs	
	—		

Put the butter and sugar into a small bowl and cream together well. Stir in the brandy.

Using a sharp knife, cut the figs into quarters and arrange in 4 individual serving dishes. Add a spoonful of the brandy butter, decorate with fresh mint leaves and serve.

festive mince pies

	ingredients	
easy	200 g/7 oz plain flour, plus extra for dusting 100 g/3½ oz butter 25 g/1 oz icing sugar 1 egg yolk 2–3 tbsp milk	300 g/10½ oz mincemeat 1 egg, beaten, for sealing and glazing icing sugar, for dusting sprigs of holly, to decorate
makes 12		
20 minutes		
15 minutes		

Preheat the oven to 180°C/350°F/Gas Mark 4. Sift the flour into a mixing bowl. Using your fingertips, rub in the butter until the mixture resembles breadcrumbs. Mix in the sugar and egg yolk. Stir in enough milk to make a soft dough, turn out onto a lightly floured work surface and knead lightly until smooth.

Shape the dough into a ball and roll out to a thickness of 1 cm/ ½ inch. Use fluted cutters to cut out 12 rounds of 7 cm/2¾ inches diameter and 12 rounds of 5 cm/2 inches diameter. Dust 12 tartlet tins with flour and line with the larger dough rounds. Prick the bases with a fork, then half-fill each pie with mincemeat. Brush beaten egg around the rims, then press the smaller dough rounds on top to seal. Make a small hole in the top of each one. Decorate the pies with Christmas trees made from dough trimmings. Brush all over with beaten egg, then bake for 15 minutes. Remove from the oven and cool on a wire rack. Dust with icing sugar, decorate and serve.

christmas cake

	ingredients	
easy	150 g/5½ oz raisins	225 g/8 oz plain flour
	125 g/4½ oz stoned dates, chopped	½ tsp salt
makes one 20-cm/8-inch cake	125 g/4½ oz sultanas	½ tsp baking powder
	100 g/3½ oz glacé cherries, rinsed	1 tsp mixed spice
	150 ml/5 fl oz brandy	25 g/1 oz toasted almonds, chopped
45 minutes, plus 8 hours to soak	225 g/8 oz butter, plus extra for greasing	25 g/1 oz toasted hazelnuts, chopped
		450 g/1 lb icing sugar
	200 g/7 oz caster sugar	1 egg white
	4 eggs	juice of 1 lemon
3 hours	grated rind of 1 orange and 1 lemon	1 tsp vanilla essence
	1 tbsp black treacle	holly leaves, to decorate

Make this cake at least 3 weeks in advance. Put all the fruit in a bowl, pour over the brandy and soak overnight.

Preheat the oven to 110°C/225°F/Gas Mark ¼. Grease a 20-cm/ 8-inch cake tin and line it with greaseproof paper. In a bowl, cream together the butter and sugar until fluffy. Gradually beat in the eggs. Stir in the citrus rind and black treacle. In a separate bowl, sift together the flour, salt, baking powder and mixed spice, then fold into the egg mixture. Fold in the fruit, brandy and nuts, then spoon into the cake tin. Bake for at least 3 hours. If it browns too quickly, cover with foil. The cake is cooked when a skewer inserted into the centre comes out clean. Remove from the oven and cool on a wire rack. Store in an airtight container until required.

To make the icing, put the sugar, egg white, lemon juice and vanilla into a bowl and mix until smooth. Spread over the cake, using a fork to give texture. Decorate with holly leaves.

brandy & orange ice cream

		ingredients
easy	4 egg yolks	DECORATION
	100 g/3½ oz caster sugar	finely sliced starfruit
serves 4	200ml/7 fl oz milk	crystallised orange peel
	250 ml/9 fl oz double cream	
	3 tbsp orange juice	
25–40 minutes + 1¾–4 hours to freeze	3 tbsp brandy	
	1 tbsp finely grated orange rind	
5 minutes		

Beat the egg yolks and sugar together in a heatproof bowl until fluffy. Put the milk, cream, orange juice, brandy and grated orange rind into a large saucepan and bring to the boil. Remove from the heat and whisk into the beaten egg yolks. Return the mixture to the pan and cook, stirring constantly, over a very low heat until thickened. Do not let it simmer. Remove from the heat, transfer to a bowl and cool. Cover with clingfilm and chill for 1 hour.

Transfer the mixture to an ice cream maker and process for 15 minutes. Alternatively, put the mixture into a freezerproof container and freeze for 1 hour. Transfer to a bowl and beat to break up the ice crystals, then put it back in the freezerproof container and freeze for 30 minutes. Repeat twice more, whisking each time and freezing for 30 minutes. Freeze until ready to serve.

To serve, soften in the refrigerator for 20 minutes beforehand. Scoop into dishes and decorate with starfruit and orange peel.

candied fruit ice cream

very easy	
serves 4	
20 minutes + 4–5 hours to freeze	
—	

ingredients

75 g/2¾ oz sultanas
75 g/2¾ oz raisins
6 tbsp almond liqueur, such
   as Amaretto
4 eggs, separated
100 g/3½ oz caster sugar
600 ml/1 pint double cream

100 g/3½ oz glacé cherries
50 g/1¾ oz crystallised citrus peel
70 g/2½ oz blanched almonds,
   chopped

strips of crystallised peel, to decorate

Put the sultanas and raisins in a bowl and pour over 4 tablespoons of almond liqueur. Cover with clingfilm and leave to soak.

Beat the egg yolks and sugar together in a large bowl until fluffy. In a separate bowl, whisk together the cream and remaining almond liqueur, then whisk the mixture into the beaten egg yolks. In a separate bowl, whisk the egg whites until stiff peaks form, then fold into the cream mixture along with the soaked fruit, cherries, citrus peel and chopped almonds.

Transfer the mixture into a heatproof pudding basin, cover and freeze for 4–5 hours until set. To serve, dip the pudding basin in hot water to loosen the ice cream, then turn it out onto a serving plate. Decorate with strips of crystallised peel and serve.

white chocolate truffles

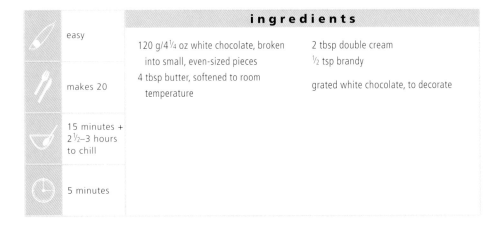

easy	
makes 20	
15 minutes + 2½–3 hours to chill	
5 minutes	

ingredients

120 g/4¼ oz white chocolate, broken into small, even-sized pieces

4 tbsp butter, softened to room temperature

2 tbsp double cream

½ tsp brandy

grated white chocolate, to decorate

Put the chocolate pieces into a heatproof glass bowl and place over a pan of hot but not simmering water. When it starts to melt, stir gently until completely melted. Do not overheat, or the chocolate will separate. Remove from the heat and gently stir in the butter, then the cream and brandy. Leave to cool, then cover with clingfilm and refrigerate for 2–2½ hours until set.

Remove the chocolate mixture from the refrigerator. Using a teaspoon, scoop out small pieces of the mixture, then use your hands to roll them into balls. To decorate, roll the balls in grated white chocolate. To store, transfer to an airtight container and refrigerate for up to 12 days.

spiced hot chocolate

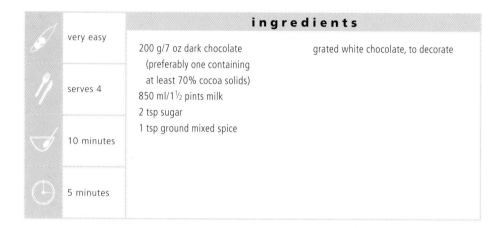

very easy	
serves 4	
10 minutes	
5 minutes	

ingredients

200 g/7 oz dark chocolate
  (preferably one containing
  at least 70% cocoa solids)
850 ml/1 ½ pints milk
2 tsp sugar
1 tsp ground mixed spice

grated white chocolate, to decorate

Break the chocolate into small, even-sized pieces. Put the milk, chocolate, sugar and mixed spice into a saucepan over a medium heat. Whisk, stirring constantly, until the chocolate has melted and the mixture is simmering but not boiling.

Remove from the heat and pour into heatproof glasses. Sprinkle over some grated white chocolate and serve.

mulled wine

			ingredients	
	extremely easy	750 ml/1⅓ pints of red wine	½ tsp ground mixed spice	
		3 tbsp sherry	2 tbsp clear honey	
	serves 4	8 cloves	1 seedless orange, cut into wedges	
		1 cinnamon stick	1 lemon, cut into wedges	
	5–10 minutes			
	5–10 minutes			

Put the wine, sherry, cloves, cinnamon, mixed spice and honey into a saucepan and stir together well. Warm over a low heat, stirring, until just starting to simmer, but do not let it boil. Remove from the heat and strain through a sieve. Discard the cloves and cinnamon stick.

Return the wine to the pan with the orange and lemon wedges. Warm gently over a very low heat, but do not let it boil. Remove from the heat, pour into heatproof glasses and serve hot.

christmas punch

	ingredients	
extremely easy	1 litre/1¾ pints of red wine	100 ml/3½ fl oz orange liqueur, such
	4 tbsp sugar	as Cointreau
	1 cinnamon stick	2 seedless oranges, cut into wedges
serves 10	400 ml/14 fl oz boiling water	2 dessert apples, cored and cut
	100 ml/3½ fl oz brandy	into wedges
	100 ml/3½ fl oz sherry	
10 minutes		
5–10 minutes		

Put the wine, sugar and cinnamon into a large saucepan and stir together well. Warm over a low heat, stirring, until just starting to simmer, but do not let it boil. Remove from the heat and strain through a sieve. Discard the cinnamon stick.

Return the wine to the pan and stir in the water, brandy, sherry and orange liqueur. Add the orange and apple wedges and warm gently over a very low heat, but do not let it boil. Remove from the heat and pour into a large, heatproof punch-bowl. Ladle into heatproof glasses and serve hot.

index